World Soccer Stars / Estrellas del fútbol mundial™

Rafael Márquez

Arturo Contró

English translation: Megan Benson

PowerKiDS press™

Editorial Buenas Letras™
New York

Published in 2008 by The Rosen Publishing Group, Inc.
29 East 21st Street, New York, NY 10010

First Edition
Book Design: Nelson Sa

Cataloging Data

Contró, Arturo, 1967-
Rafael Márquez / Arturo Contró; English translation: Megan Benson — 1st ed.
p.cm. – (World Soccer Stars / Estrellas del fútbol mundial).
Includes Index.
ISBN: 978-1-4042-7667-3
1. Márquez, Rafael–Juvenile literature. 2. Soccer players–Biography–Juvenile literature. 3. Spanish-language materials.

Manufactured in the United States of America

Photo Credits: Cover (left) © John MacDougall/Getty Images; cover (right) © Behrouz Mehri/Getty Images; p. 5 © Valery Hache/Getty Images; p. 7 © Vince Bucci/Getty Images; p. 9 © Shaun Botterill/Getty Images; p. 11 © Javier Soriano/Getty Images; p. 13 © Alex Livesey/Getty Images; pp. 15, 19 © Daniel Garcia/Getty Images; pp. 17, 21 © Cesar Rangel/Getty Images.

Contents

Contenido

Rafael Márquez is a Mexican soccer player. He is known as Rafa Márquez. Rafa was born on February 13, 1979, in Zamora, Michoacán, Mexico.

Rafael Márquez es un futbolista mexicano. Se le conoce como "Rafa" Márquez. Rafa nació el 13 de febrero de 1979, en Zamora, Michoacán.

When Rafa was 13 years old, he joined the team Atlas de Guadalajara. At 17, Rafa started playing on the **professional** team.

A los 13 años, Rafa Márquez se unió al equipo Atlas de Guadalajara. A los 17 años, Rafa comenzó a jugar en el equipo **profesional**.

MÁRQUEZ

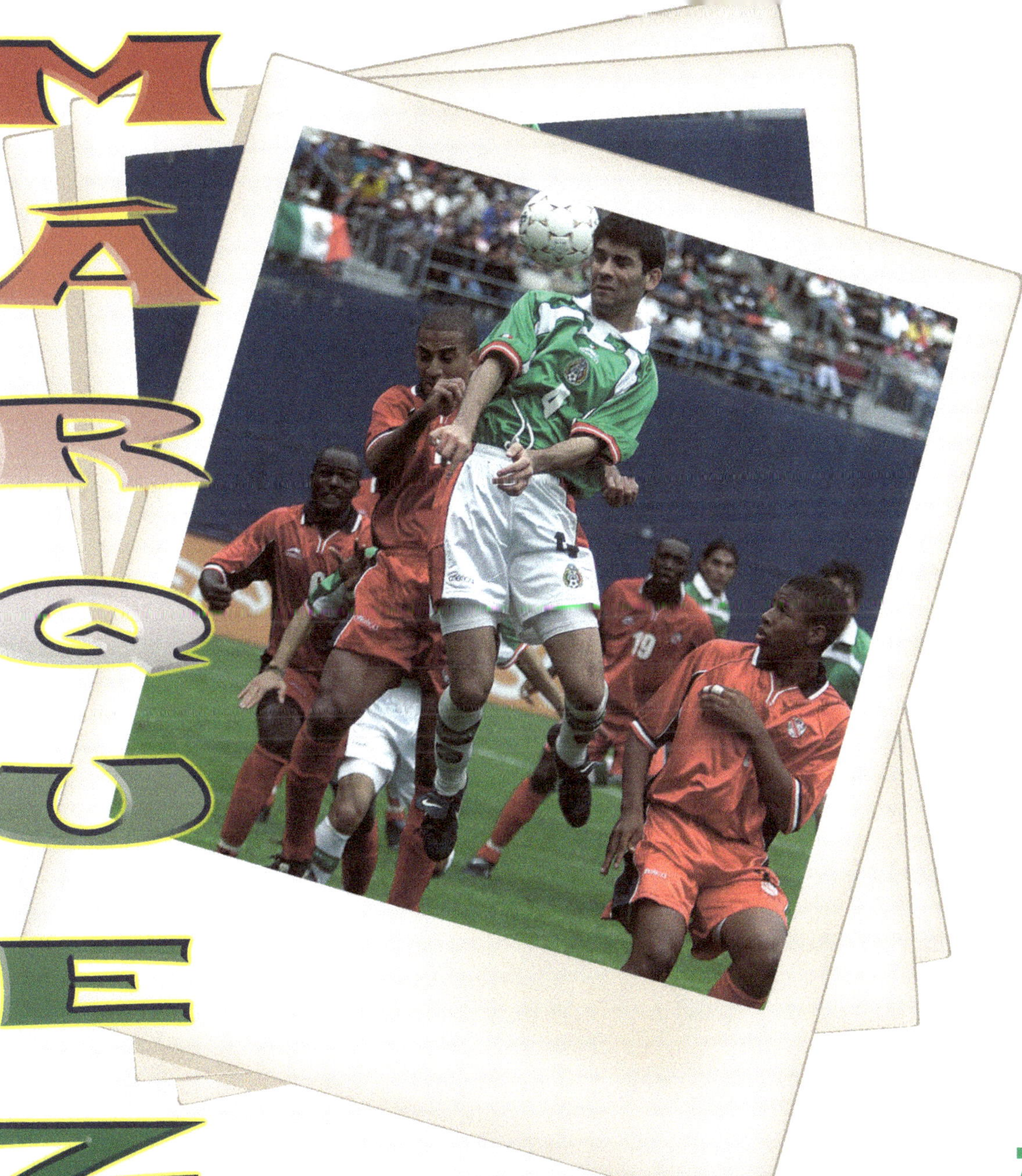

Rafa Márquez is a defender. Rafa is well known for stopping **forwards** from other teams from scoring goals.

Rafa Márquez juega como defensor. Rafa es famoso por evitar que los **delanteros** de otros equipos puedan anotar goles.

Kappa
bwin .de
10
Kappa

In 1999, Rafa went to play with the team AS Monaco. This is a French team. That year, Rafa was named the best defensive player of the year.

En 1999, Rafa empezó a jugar con el equipo AS Mónaco. El AS Mónaco es un equipo de Francia. Rafa fue campeón con el AS Mónaco y fue nombrado el mejor defensor del año.

Rafa has won many tournaments with the Mexican national team. In 1999, he helped the Mexican team win the Confederations Cup, and in 2003, the Golden Cup.

Rafa ha ganado muchos torneos con la selección de México. En 1999, Rafa ayudó al equipo mexicano a ganar la Copa Confederaciones, y en 2003, la Copa de Oro.

Rafa has played in two **World Cups**. He played in Korea/Japan in 2002 and in Germany in 2006. In both, Rafa was the team captain for the Mexican national team.

Rafa ha jugado dos **Copas del Mundo**. Rafa jugó en Corea/Japón 2002 y en Alemania 2006. En las dos copas Rafa fue el capitán de la selección de México.

adidas
19

In 2003, Rafa joined Barcelona, in Spain. With Barcelona, Rafa has won two Spanish championships. He also helped Barcelona win the European championship.

En 2003, Rafa se unió al Barcelona de España. Con el Barcelona, Rafa ha sido campeón de España dos veces. Rafa también ayudó al Barcelona a ganar el Campeonato de Europa.

Although he plays as a defender, Rafa also scores goals. He scored an important goal against Argentina during the World Cup Germany 2006.

Aunque juega de defensa, Rafa también mete goles. Uno de sus goles más importantes lo anotó contra Argentina en el mundial de Alemania 2006.

Rafa does more than just play soccer. He also runs a **foundation** called Rafa Márquez: Game and Spirit. With the foundation, Rafa helps poor children eat better, study, and enjoy soccer.

Además de jugar fútbol, Rafa ayuda a los niños con la **fundación** Rafa Márquez: Fútbol y Corazón. Esta fundación ayuda a los niños pobres para que coman mejor, estudien y disfruten del fútbol.

ZONA 2
SAVIOLA
7

Glossary / Glosario

forwards (**for**-werdz) Players who try to score goals.

foundation (found-**day**-shun) A group that works to help others.

professional (pruh-**fesh**-nul) Somebody making money for doing something.

World Cups (**wur**-uld **kups**) A soccer tournament that takes place every four years with teams from around the world.

Copa del Mundo (la) Torneo de fútbol en el que juegan los mejores equipos del mundo.

delanteros (los) Jugadores que tienen la función de anotar goles.

fundación (la) Grupo de personas que trabajan para ayudar a otras personas.

profesional Una persona que gana dinero realizando alguna actividad.

Resources / Recursos

Books in English/Libros en inglés

Otten, Jack. Soccer. New York: PowerKids Press, 2002

Books in Spanish/Libros en español

Page, Jason. El fútbol. Minneapolis: Two-Can Publishers, 2001

Web Sites

Due to the changing nature of Internet links, The Rosen Publishing Group has developed an online list of Web sites related to the subject of this book. This site is updated regularly. Please use this link to access the list:

www.buenasletraslinks.com/ss/marquez

Index

Índice